MOUNTAINS

MOUNTAINS

GREAT PEAKS AND RANGES OF THE WORLD

CHRIS McNAB

amber
BOOKS

This Amber edition first published in 2023.

Published by Amber Books Ltd
United House
North Road
London
N7 9DP
United Kingdom

www.amberbooks.co.uk
Instagram: amberbooksltd
Facebook: amberbooks
Twitter: @amberbooks
Pinterest: amberbooksltd

ISBN: 978-1-83886-312-8

Project Editor: Anna Brownbridge
Designer: Keren Harragan
Picture Research: Terry Forshaw

Printed in China

Contents

Introduction

Mountains are the most enduring monuments to the slow violence of Earth's geological evolution. Over tens of millions of years, volcanic, tectonic and erosive activity have laboured to create these giant, steep-sided landscapes of rock, the jagged peaks often collected in huge mountain ranges that extend across hundreds or even thousands of miles.

Where a hill ends and a mountain begins is a matter of argument. Some define mountains as those with elevations of more than 300m (984ft), whereas others demand at least double that height for them to be on the list. There are also geological distinctions made between mountains, massifs and volcanoes. Yet at the level of popular understanding, most of us know a mountain when we see one. As the photographs in this book illustrate, mountains cast psychological impressions as great as their physical shadows. They are features of astonishing and towering beauty, their silhouettes etched against rarefied air. They can be deeply hostile to human visitors, killing dozens of climbers and trekkers every year through falls, landslides, avalanches, altitude sickness and a host of other lethal effects. Nonetheless, for those who dare to summit mountains, or even for the many who simply look up at their peaks from below, mountains provide us with the most profound sense of being alive, our tiny frames set against the majesty and power of Earth at its most spectacular.

OPPOSITE:
Mount Rainier, Cascade Range, Washington State, USA
The highest mountain in the Cascade Range in western North America, Mount Rainier is actually a heavily glaciated volcano, climbed by 8000–13,000 people every year.

Europe

A casual glance at a topographical map of Europe quickly illustrates the fact that mountainous terrain covers much of the continent. The flat northern European plain is effectively sandwiched between broad and long mountain chains. To the north are the Scottish Highlands and the Scandinavian mountains, the latter running through, indeed dominating, Finland, Norway and Sweden. These mountains are not lofty in comparative terms – Mount Galdhøpiggen in southern Norway is the highest in the chain with an elevation of 2469m (8100ft) – yet they form some of Europe's most spectacular scenery. To the south, we see a band of mountain chains running almost unbroken from the Atlantic coast to the Black Sea. The Pyrenees of the northern Iberian peninsular merge into the majestic Alps, one of the world's greatest displays of geology, with the mighty Carpathians taking over in eastern Europe. Most of Iberia, Italy and the Balkans are also internally mountainous. Looking across the Black Sea and further east, the Caucasus Mountains (which include Europe's highest peak, Mount Elbrus) and the Urals effectively form the elevated frontiers between Europe and Asia. Consequently, although Europe's history has been shaped by its coasts and seas, mountains have also framed its environmental and cultural evolution.

OPPOSITE:
Ben Nevis, Scottish Highlands, Scotland
Once an active volcano towering over the Scottish Grampians, Ben Nevis today stands as the highest mountain in the British Isles, at 1344.5m (4411ft). The summit is attainable by hiking, hence the mountain attracts more than 125,000 walkers every year.

RIGHT:

Navigational Cairns, Ben Nevis, Scottish Highlands, Scotland
The navigational cairns on Ben Nevis provide a useful landmark for thousands of walkers and climbers who ascend the mountain partially or completely every year. On a clear day, those stood at the top of the mountain can see across 190km (120 miles) of distance, looking across the spectacular scenery of the north-west Highlands.

OPPOSITE TOP:

North Face of Ben Nevis, Scottish Highlands, Scotland
The north face of Ben Nevis is an imposing and jagged granite wall, riven with fissures. For climbers rather than hikers, it is a popular challenge, particularly the 600m (1968ft) Tower Route that leads up to Tower Ridge. For hikers, the summit ridges of the north face can be reached by walking up the western slopes.

OPPOSITE BOTTOM:

Red Deer Stag, Ben Nevis, Scottish Highlands, Scotland
A magnificent red deer stag presents itself on the skyline on Ben Nevis. The mountain and its surrounding environs have rich wildlife, including pine martens, snow buntings, ptarmigans and water voles, plus soaring golden and white-tailed eagles. Butterflies proliferate in the summer, including rare types such as the mountain ringlet and chequered skipper.

Nevis Gorge, Ben Nevis, Scottish Highlands, Scotland
The Nevis Gorge winds its way around the base of Ben Nevis, not only providing great views of the mountain above, but also taking the walker through diverse countryside that ranges from picturesque to imposing. The gorge boasts some particularly ancient woodlands, rich in alder, ash, aspen, birch, elm and Scots pine trees, plus numerous species of flowers and lichen (the latter including 33 rare species).

ABOVE:

Mount Snowdon / Yr Wyddfa
Snowdonia, Wales
Known in Welsh as Yr Wyddfa
(pronounced 'Ur Oy-thfa'),
Mount Snowdon is the highest
mountain in Wales, reaching an
altitude of 1085m (3560ft). The
mountain has extremely high
levels of precipitation, with more
than 5100mm (200in) of rain or
snow every year.

RIGHT:

Llyn Llydaw,
Mount Snowdon / Yr Wyddfa
Snowdonia, Wales
Mount Snowdon has been
sculpted by glaciation over
millennia, forming many
cwms (rounded valleys) in the
surrounding landscape. The
lake visible here on Snowdon's eastern
cwm is Llyn Llydaw, which has
waters reaching to depths of
58m (190ft) in parts.

Kirkjufell, Snæfellsnes Peninsula, Iceland
Mirrored perfectly in the lake at its base, Kirkjufell (Church Mountain) is popularly regarded as the most photographed mountain in Iceland. It has even achieved fame on-screen, appearing in the HBO TV series *Game of Thrones*, in which it epitomizes the harsh but beautiful landscape beyond 'The Wall'.

OPPOSITE TOP:

Mount Ahkka, Stora Sjöfallet National Park, Sweden
The poetic beauty of Sweden's Mount Ahkka is captured in this early morning photograph. The massif has 11 peaks in total, the highest of which, Stortoppen, has an elevation of 2015m (6611ft) and a precipitous vertical drop from its summit. The mountain is often referred to as the 'Queen of Lapland'.

OPPOSITE BOTTOM:

Mount Galdhøpiggen, Innlandet, Norway
The highest mountain in northern Europe at 2469m (8100ft), Galdhøpiggen (meaning 'The peak of the Galdhø mountain') is located in south-central Norway and is part of the Jotunheimen mountainous area. Previously, nearby Mount Glittertind took the crown as Norway's highest mountain, but the shrinkage of the glacier at its peak meant that it has dropped fractionally lower than Galdhøpiggen.

ABOVE:

Trollveggen, Trolltindene, Norway
The Trollveggen (Troll Wall) is a towering spur of rock, part of the Store Trolltind mountain in the Romsdalen valley of western Norway. From the base of the rock to the summit the drop is 1100m (3608ft), which makes the Trollveggen the tallest vertical and overhanging rock face in Europe. As such, Trollvegen is popular with thrill-seeking base jumpers, as well as expert climbers.

ABOVE:
Ibex, Mont Blanc, Alps
An ibex stands on mighty Mont Blanc. The highest mountain in both the Alps and in Western Europe, Mont Blanc reaches a height of 4808m (15,774ft).

LEFT:
Mont Blanc, Alps
Mont Blanc's awe-inspiring beauty attracts many climbers and hikers. However, the mountain is also known for its dangers, with accidents, rockfalls and unstable snow structures claiming multiple lives every year.

OPPOSITE:
Kirkjufell, Snæfellsnes Peninsula, Iceland
Located on the north coast of the Snæfellsnes Peninsula, Kirkjufell is 463m (1519ft) tall at its summit. It is a 'nunatuk', a mountain that lifted above a surrounding glacier during the Ice Age.

Mont Blanc Massif, Alps
The Mont Blanc Massif, to
which the Mont Blanc mountain
gives its name, has 11 individual
summits. At 46km (29 miles)
long and 20km (12 miles) wide,
the massif straddles parts of
France, Italy and Switzerland and
is extensively covered in glaciers,
although the retreat of those
glaciers is a concerning measure
of rapid environmental change.

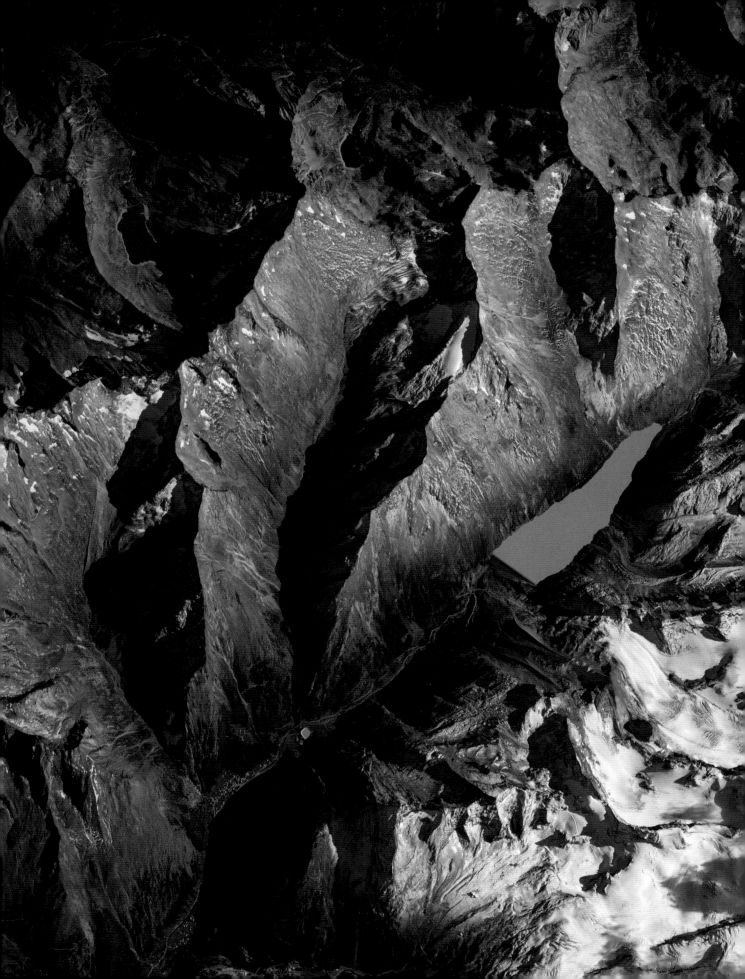

Mattmarksee Reservoir, Swiss Alps
A satellite photograph of the Alps provides a god's eye view of their scale and environmental range. In total, the Alps stretch 1200km (750 miles) in length from the Mediterranean coast of France in the west to Austria in the east, the chain measuring up to 200km (125 miles) deep in parts. Although the Alps cross through numerous countries, only Switzerland and Austria are considered true Alpine countries.

OPPOSITE:
Edelweiss Flower, The Alps
Edelweiss is the quintessential symbol of the Alps and grows only at high altitudes of 1500–3000m (3280–9850ft). The Alps are renowned for their rich and often rare varieties of flowering plants.

LEFT:
Golden Eagle, The Alps
The Alps have the world's largest population of golden eagles. These awe-inspiring birds can have wingspans up to 2.3m (7ft 6in) that enable them to soar effortlessly over Alpine pastures, hunting creatures such as ibexes, squirrels, foxes and rabbits.

BELOW:
The Alps
The Alps have a strong pastoral tradition of transhumance – the seasonal droving of livestock. Herders drove alpine cows, such as this fine example, between lowland valleys in the winter and higher mountain pastures in the summer where there is more food available for grazing.

Dufourspitze, Alps
Dufourspitze is the second highest mountain in the Alps, after Mont Blanc. Here, pictured flowing around its summit, is the Gorner glacier to the left and the Grenz glacier on the right. A line of moraine (rocky material deposited by glacial movement) demarcates the meeting of the two glaciers.

Grossglockner, High Tauern National Park, Austria
Climbers move carefully along a ridgeline towards the summit of the Grossglockner, the highest mountain in Austria at 3798m (12,460ft). The mountain is located in Austria's High Tauern National Park, which contains more than 200 peaks over the 3000m (9842ft) mark, together with 382 glaciers.

ABOVE TOP:

Alpine Ibex, High Tauern National Park, Austria

The Alpine ibex is an exceptional animal capable of surviving in high-altitude environments that are for much of the year above the snow line, although it moves to lower slopes in winter. A superb climber, it can ascend near-vertical slopes of sheer rock.

ABOVE BOTTOM:

Pasterze, High Tauern National Park, Austria

The High Tauern is actually a lengthy mountain chain within the Alps, separated into various sub-groups of peaks. Of the numerous glaciers in the park, the 8-km (5-mile) long Pasterze is the longest, here seen with the Grossglockner massif on its left.

RIGHT:

High Tauern National Park, Austria

The High Tauern National Park has around 350 alpine pastures and is home to an estimated 3500 species of plant. Summertime visitors to the region are frequently impressed by the strong floral scents present in the pure mountain air.

LEFT:
Matterhorn, Switzerland / Italy
The four-sided pyramidal lines of the Matterhorn have made this mountain an iconic landmark. However, at an elevation of 4478m (14,691ft) it is one that still challenges professional climbers. Its distinctive shape was formed through millions of years of glacial movement and weathering erosion.

ABOVE TOP:
Mount Olympus, Pieria, Greece
A spectacular sunset view from Mount Olympus. The mountain has 52 peaks, the highest of which, at 2917m (9570ft), makes Olympus Greece's highest mountain. The mountain is thought to be the home of the ancient Olympian gods, which places it at the mythical heart of Greek history.

ABOVE BOTTOM:
Balkan Chamois, Mount Olympus, Pieria, Greece
The Balkan chamois is just one of many different animal species that live on the slopes of Mount Olympus. Other significant mammal species on the mountain include wild boars, wild cats and red foxes, along with rare species of reptile and birds of prey.

Mytikas Peak, Mount Olympus, Pieria, Greece
The Mytikas peak ridgeline of Mount Olympus takes a slice out of the blue Grecian sky. Olympus is a hikeable mountain, although that feat typically takes about two days for experienced hikers, including a night spent in one of the mountain's refuges.

ABOVE TOP:

North Face, Tre Cime di Lavaredo Dolomites, Italy
From east to west, the Tre Cime di Lavaredo consist of three peaks: the Cima Piccola ('little peak'), Cima Grande ('big peak') and Cima Ovest ('western peak'). This photograph shows the north faces of the peaks and dramatically captures the last rays of a sunset to the west.

ABOVE BOTTOM:

Tre Cime di Lavaredo Dolomites, Italy
Although the Tre Cime di Lavaredo look uninhabitable, during World War I the mountains formed part of the high-altitude battlefield for the conflict between the Italians and the Austro-Hungarians. Many fortifications and outposts still remain visible today.

RIGHT:

Routes of Tre Cime di Lavaredo Dolomites, Italy
In addition to the hiking routes around the three mountains, the Tre Cime di Lavaredo also offer several challenging climbs that typically take 6–10 hours depending on the chosen route. The friable nature of the limestone means it can be a dangerous climb.

Mount Aragats, Lesser Caucasus, Armenia
Mount Aragats is a powerful massif in Armenia; its four peaks were created by prehistoric volcanic activity, with the crater forming the basin for a glacier. The highest point of the mountain has an elevation of 4090m (13,418ft), towering above the picturesque Ararat Plain to the south.

LEFT:

Mount Elbrus, Caucasus, Russia
Elbrus is the highest mountain in
Europe, with a western summit
at 5643m (18,513ft) elevation
and an eastern summit at 5621m
(18,442ft). Both of the summits
are dormant volcanoes, situated
1.5km (0.9 miles) apart. Weather
conditions on the mountain are
ferocious, especially in winter,
and 15–30 mountaineers are
killed on Elbrus every year.

ALL PHOTOGRAPHS ABOVE:

**Mount Shkhara, Caucasus,
Georgia**
Part of the Bezingi massif that
stretches 12km (7.5 miles)
through the Caucasus mountain
chain, Mount Shkhara is the
third highest mountain in the
Caucasus with a height of
5193m (17,037ft). First ascended
in 1888, the mountain is known
to be a challenging as well as
dangerous climb.

OPPOSITE:

Mount Shkhara, Caucasus, Georgia
A broad glacier runs down from the peaks of Mount Shkara. In total, the mountain has nine summits and is considered one of the most demanding technical climbs in Europe, with 10 of the climbing routes classed in the highest grades of difficulty.

LEFT:

Mount Triglav, Julian Alps, Slovenia
The highest mountain in Slovenia (and the former Yugoslavia), Mount Triglav has an elevation of 2864m (9396ft). At the summit is a storm shelter and triangulation point known as the Aljaž Tower.

BELOW:

Mount Triglav, Julian Alps, Slovenia
Mount Triglav provides spellbinding views over Triglav National Park, which covers an area of 880 sq km (340 sq miles). The mountain is regarded as a symbol of Slovenian identity and is depicted on the nation's coat of arms.

View from the Summit, Mount Triglav, Julian Alps, Slovenia
The view from the summit of Mount Triglav shows the panorama of the Julian Alps. The chain stretches from north-eastern Italy to near Ljubljana in Slovenia, and the mountains therein are mainly of limestone. The area is a tourist hotspot in the summer, and popular with skiers in the winter.

Asia & Pacific

Collectively, Asia and the Pacific cover approximately 60 per cent of the Earth's surface. Across that vast swathe of terrestrial and aquatic territory, it is possible to journey through every conceivable kind of terrain, from silent deserts and frozen tundra to tropical jungles and temperate lowlands. It is also in Asia that we encounter the world's loftiest mountains. When we think of Asian mountain chains, we instinctively think of the Himalayas. This vast, arcing range, running from Afghanistan in the west to Bhutan in the east, has more than 100 peaks exceeding 7200m (23,600ft), including the world's highest mountain – Mount Everest.

The Himalayas are framed by nearby chains of near-equal majesty, including the Hindu Kush, Karakoram, Pamir and Tien Shan. Yet the eye-catching headlines of mountainous east Asia can distract us from the other exceptional ranges and peaks within the continent. Indonesia, for example, is punctuated by volcanic mountains as beautiful as they are periodically dangerous. The Middle East has mountains steeped in theological history, such as Mount Hermon in Syria. Japan's mountains lie at the heart of its spiritual traditions and national identity. Almost every Asian country has its mountain peaks, and each one has its own spiritual, political and sporting stories to tell.

OPPOSITE:
Iran–Pakistan border
Many of the boundaries between Asian states are both defined and blurred by mountainous terrain. Occaisonally, as in the case of the border territories between India and China, these porous regions become politically and militarily contested.

RIGHT TOP:

Mount Jebel Shams, Hajar Range, Oman

With a north summit at an elevation of 3009m (9872ft), Mount Jebel Shams in north-eastern Oman has stunning views across the surrounding Al Nakhur Canyon, also known as the 'Grand Canyon of Arabia'.

RIGHT BOTTOM:

Qurnat as Sawda', Lebanon Mountains, Lebanon

Qurnat as Sawda' is Lebanon's highest peak, at 3088m (10,131ft). The mountain is part of the Lebanon Mountains range that runs through the centre of the country parallel to the Mediterranean coast.

OPPOSITE:

Mount Ararat, Turkey

Mount Ararat has an assured place in human history. According to legend, it is regarded as the place on which Noah's Ark came to rest after the Great Flood recounted in the book of Genesis. It is a two-peak mountain, with the highest peak – Great Ararat (pictured here) – reaching 5165m (16,945ft).

Karakorum Range
Here, observed from the vantage point of a satellite in low-Earth orbit, the Karakorum mountain range crosses the borders of Pakistan, India and China, stretching more than 500km (311 miles). It includes K2, the world's second highest mountain at 8611m (28,251ft), but also four other peaks exceeding 8000m (26,000ft).

ABOVE TOP:
Uraman Takht, Sarvabad, Iran
The Kurdish-populated village of Uraman Takht in western Iran illustrates how human beings have been able to exist in even high-altitude locations. The terraced village faces the northern front of the Takht-e Soleyman massif, part of the Alborz mountain range.

ABOVE BOTTOM:
Mount Damavand, Alborz Mountains, Iran
The graceful lines of Mount Damavand form a peaceful backdrop for these grazing Iranian horses. Damavand is Iran's highest peak, with an elevation of 5671m (18,606ft), and sits in the Alborz range south of the Caspian Sea.

RIGHT:
Gasherbrum II, Gasherbrum massif, Karakoram
A climber trudges through deep snow as he attempts to reach the summit of Gasherbrum II, the 13th highest mountain in the world at 8035m (26,362ft). The trapezoidal mountain seen top right is Chogolisa, with an elevation of 7665m (25,148ft).

Mount Sabalan, Ardabil Province, Iran
Mount Sabalan peaks at 4794m (15,728ft) in elevation, making it Iran's third highest peak. It is actually an inactive volcano, its rugged lines built up by tens of millions of years of volcanic deposits, blasts and collapses. It is a relatively easy climb in the summer months.

Hindu Kush, Central / South Asia
Some 800km (500 miles) long
and 240km (150 miles) wide
at points, the Hindu Kush
dominates the border between
Afghanistan and Pakistan and
runs up to the Pamirs range in
Tajikistan. The valleys and
passes of the Hindu Kush,
including the famous Khyber
Pass, have been the conduits for
invading armies and marauding
bands for centuries.

Annapurna III, Annapurna massif, Himalayas, Nepal
Although the 42nd highest mountain in the world might not sound impressive, at 7555m (24,787ft) Annapurna III is still one of the great Himalayan peaks. The most challenging climb is its south-eastern route, which many failed before success finally came in 2021.

Gasherbrum II, Karakoram Range
This view across to Gasherbrum II captures the awe-inspiring vistas that are commonplace in the Karakoram range, with dozens of peaks competing to puncture the clouds above. This mountain is regarded as the easiest climb (relatively) of the 8000m (26,246ft) peaks in the range.

ABOVE:
Mount Everest, Himalayas
The highest point above sea level
on Earth, Mount Everest ascends
to a magisterial elevation at
8849m (29,032ft).

RIGHT:
**Journey to Mount Everest,
Himalayas**
Journeying to Mount Everest is
an expedition in itself. It takes
about eight days on foot and
considerable logistics to reach the
base camp, even before an ascent
of the mountain itself.

OPPOSITE TOP:
**Summit of Mount Everest,
Himalayas**
The summit of Mount Everest
penetrates the stratosphere.
It is a uniquely hostile place,
with wind speeds regularly in
excess of 160km/h (100mph).

OPPOSITE BOTTOM:
**Aerial View of Mount Everest,
Himalayas**
An aerial view of Mount Everest
reveals a foliage-like pattern
of snow-covered peaks and
snowless ridges and valleys.

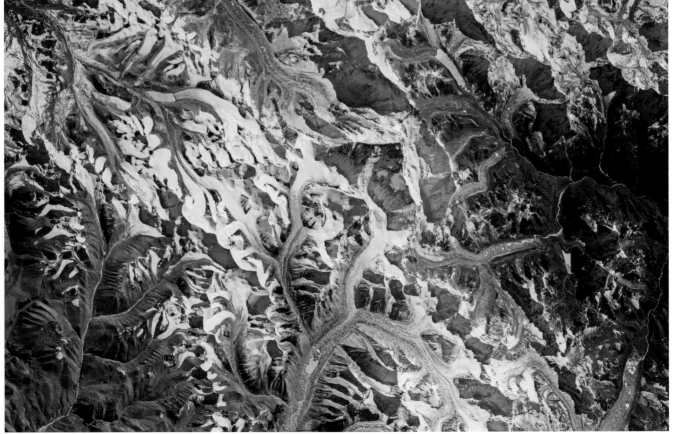

Everest Base Camp, Mount Everest, Himalayas
Everest base camp presents a windswept, untidy scene, with tents
and equipment scattered across the lower scree slopes. In recent years,
the industry that has grown around climbing Everest has attracted
controversy and debate over a range of issues, including the treatment
of Sherpa guides, the crowds forming at the summit and littering.

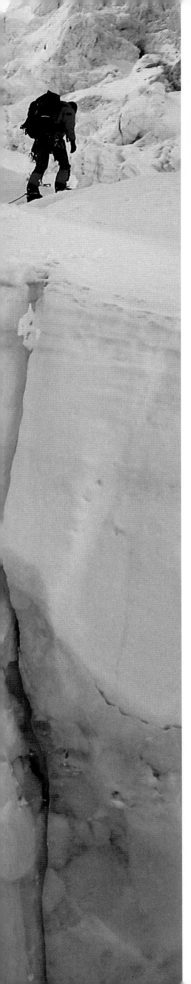

ALL PHOTOGRAPHS:
Khumbu Icefall, Mount Everest, Himalayas
The South Col route to ascend Everest takes climbers through the Khumbu Icefall, at the head of the Khumbu Glacier. It is a perilous part of the climb, the shifting ice creating deep crevasses and the ever-present threat of avalanches and ice-falls.

OVERLEAF:
Himalayas
This photograph of the Himalayas was taken from the International Space Station (ISS), as it passed over China 415km (258 miles) above Earth. Mount Everest can be seen (far right), with clouds pluming off its unrivalled summit.

Lhotse, Himalayas
Although overshadowed in the Western imagination by Everest, Lhotse is revered by professional climbers as one of the most difficult and dangerous climbs on the planet. It is the world's fourth highest mountain, with the greatest of its four summits at an elevation of 8516m (27,940ft).

RIGHT:

Lhotse, Himalayas

Lhotse stands a short distance to the south of Mount Everest, but its imposing geological formation more than holds its own against the higher mountain.

OVERLEAF:

Kumaun Himalayas, India

The Kumaun Himalayas are a 320-km (200-mile) section of the Himalayas that runs through northern India from the Kalie River in the west to the Sutlej River in the east. Here a flock of birds use its contours to navigate an ancient migratory route.

LEFT:

K2, Karakoram Range
K2 is the world's second highest mountain, reaching an elevation of 8611m (28,251ft). The first attempt to reach the summit was an Anglo-Swiss expedition in 1902, but it wasn't until 1954 that two climbers, Achille Compagnoni and Lino Lacedelli, succeeded, despite the death of one of their guides.

ABOVE TOP:

View from Base Camp, K2, Karakoram Range
A view of K2 from the base camp, with the Godwin-Austen Glacier running into the valley below. K2 is widely acknowledged as one of the world's most dangerous mountains – on average, one person dies on the mountain for every four climbers who reach the summit.

ABOVE BOTTOM:

Makalu, Khumbu Region, Nepal
Another of the Himalayan monsters, Makalu is the world's fifth-highest mountain at 8463m (27,765ft) and is located 22.5km (14 miles) east of Everest. The west face of the mountain is generally acknowledged as the most difficult route to the summit, but all routes are extremely hard, technical climbs.

Mount Hua (Hua Shan), Shaanxi Province, China
Mount Hua, despite is picturesque appearance, offers the adventurous what has been dubbed the 'world's most dangerous hiking trail.' The paths to the summit are very steep and very narrow, with lethal drops just inches from the hiker's feet. Chinese authorities have, however, made consistent efforts to improve the safety of the mountain.

LEFT:
East Peak of Mount Hua, Mount Hua (Hua Shan), Shaanxi Province, China
Like a scene from a fantasy film, the East Peak of Mount Hua rises above the clouds, its summit marked by the picturesque 'Chess Pavilion' pagoda. Regarded as one of China's sacred mountains, Mount Hua has five peaks in total, each featuring small temples, tea houses and shrines.

ABOVE TOP:
Mount Hua (Hua Shan), Shaanxi Province, China
Just one example of the vertiginous paths that wrap themselves around Mount Hua. At times, hikers will find themselves negotiating near-vertical steps or climbing precarious ladders, but there are now two cable cars offering a more relaxing route to the top.

ABOVE BOTTOM:
South Peak, Mount Hua (Hua Shan), Shaanxi Province, China
The highest of Mount Hua's summits is the South Peak, at 2155m (7070ft) in elevation. The climate around the mountain, as this picture suggests, can be hot and humid in the summer months, with high rainfall, but it plunges to well below freezing in the winter.

Mount Yari, Hida Mountains, Japan

Named after the point of a spear (*yari*), Mount Yari is a 3180m (10,433ft) peak in the Hida Mountains, a range also known as the Northern Japanese Alps. The mountain, which is the fifth-highest in Japan, is a popular destination for hikers, and a physically fit walker can reach the summit in about seven hours.

Mount Fuji, Honshu, Japan
Few mountains in the world
are as instantly recognizable as
Mount Fuji, which overlooks
Tokyo from the south-west.
The mountain is the highest
in Japan, with an elevation of
3776m (12,389ft). Mount Fuji
is an active volcano, although it
has not erupted since the Hoei
eruption of 1707–08.

Summit of Mount Fuji, Honshu, Japan

A close-up of the summit of Mount Fuji on an evidently windy day. Fuji is an iconic presence in Japanese art, literature and mythology and is listed as one of Japan's 'three holy mountains'. The summit is regarded as a sacred place, whereas the Aokigahara forest at its base is replete with folk tales and legends.

LEFT:

Mount Agung, Bali, Indonesia
The island nation of Indonesia sits squarely on the 'Pacific Ring of Fire', the name given to the geologically volatile rim of the Pacific Ocean. Indonesia has no fewer than 127 active volcanoes, with eruptions at frequent intervals. Pictured here is Mount Agung, which at 3031m (9944ft) is the highest point on the island of Bali.

ABOVE TOP:

Mount Agung, Bali, Indonesia
Mount Agung is technically classified as a stratovolcano, one that has been built up over ages by successive strata of lava and other volcanic deposits. The shape and height of the mountain are in constant evolution. Eruptions in 2017–19 spewed out millions of tons of ash and the mountain experiences regular ground-shifting earthquakes.

ABOVE BOTTOM:

Summit of Mount Agung, Bali, Indonesia
The summit of Mount Agung is a four to seven-hour hike from the mountain's base, depending on the route chosen and the hiker's physical fitness. Locals treat the mountain with reverence, regarding it as the 'navel of the world', and craft religious artefacts in its distinctive shape. In Balinese mythology, Agung is the home of its deities.

Mount Agung, Bali, Indonesia
Plumes of steam remind us that Mount Agung is an active volcano.
It is also a periodically dangerous one – its 1963 eruption killed
1600 people and left 83,000 homeless.

LEFT:

Mount Merapi, Java, Indonesia
Another of Indonesia's great volcanic mountains, Mount Merapi ('Mountain of Fire') is located on the island of Java, about 32km (20 miles) north of Yogyakarta.

OVERLEAF LEFT TOP:

Mount Merapi, Java, Indonesia
This view of Mount Merapi indicates the violence of its eruptions, which are often accompanied by lethal pyroclastic flows. One such flow in 1996 killed 64 people.

OVERLEAF LEFT BOTTOM:

Slopes of Mount Merapi, Java, Indonesia
Lava pumps down the slopes of Mount Merapi. On average, the volcano has minor eruptions every two to three years, but larger ones every 10–15 years.

OVERLEAF RIGHT:

Mount Rinjani, Lombok, Indonesia
At 3726m (12,224ft), Mount Rinjani is the second-highest volcano in Indonesia. It is highly active, with regular eruptions and earthquakes, however, the fertility of the volcanic soils on its lowlands has attracted both inhabitants and agriculture.

Segara Anak, Lombok, Indonesia
Located 2004m (6575ft) above sea level, the Segara Anak ('Child of the Sea') is a lake that nestles in the caldera next to Mount Rinjani. It was formed during the explosive eruption of Lombok's Mount Samalas in 1257. Segara Anak's name derives from the way the lake appears the same rich blue colour as the surrounding ocean.

Mount Tambora, Sumbawa, Indonesia
On 5 April 1815, Mount Tambora was the site of the largest volanic eruption in recorded history. The explosion was heard more than 2000km (1242 miles) away and the volume of ash pumped into the atmosphere lowered global temperatures for more than a year, causing crop failures in Europe. An estimated 71,000 people died in the initial eruption, but countless others died from subsequent famine.

Mount Kinabalu, Sabah, Malaysia
The view from the black granite plateau block of Mount Kinabalu. Gunung Kinabalu, as it is called in the Malay langauge, is a vast elevation on the island of Borneo in Malaysia. At 4095m (13,435ft) elevation, it is the world's third-highest island mountain peak, after Puncak Jaya in New Guinea and Mauna Kea in Hawaii.

RIGHT:

Mount Khan Tengri, Tian Shan Range, Kazakhstan
Although much of Kazakhstan consists of seemingly endless flat steppe, the Tian Shan Range runs through its southern territories on its 2500-km (1500-mile) journey across central Asia. Mount Khan Tengri is the highest mountain in Kazakhstan, at 6995m (22,949ft).

BELOW:

Mount Fansipan, Hoang Lien Son Range, Vietnam
Set in a verdant green tropical landscape, Mount Fansipan is the highest mountain in the Indochinese Peninsula (Vietnam, Laos, Thailand). A cable car now runs to the summit from the valley below.

OPPOSITE:

Khüiten Peak, Altai Range, China / Mongolia
The border between China and Mongolia cuts across the summit of this 4356m (14,291ft) mountain in the Altai Range. The peak is one of five in a massif known as the Tavan Bogd.

Aoraki / Mount Cook, Southern Alps, New Zealand
Aoraki / Mount Cook is New Zealand's highest mountain, its High Peak (the mountain has three peaks in total) having an elevation of 3724m (12,218ft). The mountain is located in the Aoraki / Mount Cook National Park, which has 23 peaks over 3000m (9842ft).

OPPOSITE:

Mount Tasman, Southern Alps, New Zealand

New Zealand's second-highest mountain, Mount Tasman, sits in the Aoraki / Mount Cook National Park. It summits at 3497m (11,473ft) and is regarded as a particularly challenging and icy climb.

LEFT:

Mauna Kea, Hawaii

Topped by mighty cinder cones, Mauna Kea is a majestic dormant volcano, its last eruption being approximately 4500 years ago. At 4205m (13796ft) elevation, it is the second-highest island peak on Earth.

BELOW:

Mount Hallasan, South Korea

Mount Hallasan is a relatively low-profile volcano on Jeju Island off the southern coast of mainland South Korea. It has an elevation of 1947m (6388ft). Here we see its crater lake (at this time largely dried up) known as *Baengnokdam*, meaning 'White Deer Lake'.

Africa

Africa is a continent usually more associated with flat expanses of desert, jungle and grassland than with towering mountains. Yet Africa's astonishing geological breadth includes mountain ranges and individual peaks of international renown that prove beguiling to the climber or trekker. Tropical explosions of wildlife and plants proliferate around the lower mountainous slopes, contrasting with sunbaked, mist-wrapped valleys below the summits. The continent is also home to what may be the planet's oldest mountain range: the Barberton Mountains in South Africa have been dated to 3.5 billion years before humans ever arrived on the scene.

Africa's great mountain ranges include the Atlas Mountains that cross Morocco, Algeria and Tunisia; the Ethiopian Highlands; the Nuba Mountains of Sudan and the Ruwenzori Mountains of the Democratic Republic of Congo (DRC) and Uganda; the latter country is also home to the Virunga Range. Africa's most famous peak is undoubtedly Kilimanjaro in Tanzania and is Africa's contribution to the 'Seven Summits' list, the highest mountains on each of the world's continents. Many of Africa's mountains can be hiked by athletic trekkers, but regardless of the elevation the rich ecology and green-carpeted vistas also deliver unforgettable experiences.

OPPOSITE:
Mount Toubkal, Atlas Mountains, Morocco
The highest peak in the Atlas Mountains, Mount Toubkal peaks at 4167m (13,671ft). It is usually ascended by trekkers rather than climbers, with a guided hike to the summit typically taking two days.

Mount Toubkal, Atlas Mountains, Morocco
A panoramic view of Mount Toubkal and the surronding Atlas Mountains. The Atlas range extends 2000km (1200 miles) through Morocco, Algeria and Tunisia, and effectively separates the North African coastline from the Sahara Desert to the south.

ABOVE:

Gelada Baboon, Simien Mountains, Ethiopian Highlands, Ethiopia
The gelada baboon is a signature animal of the Ethiopian Highlands, known grandly as the 'Roof of Africa'. Found nowhere else in the world, it lives tenaciously at elevations of 1800–4400m (5,900–14,400ft). The Ethiopian Highlands are a highly mountainous region of north-west Africa.

RIGHT:

Simien Mountains, Ethiopian Highlands, Ethiopia
Formed by lava outpourings and more than 20 million years of erosion, the Simien Mountains are today a luscious tropical habitat, but one that also experiences regular snowfall. The range includes the highest peak in Ethiopia, Ras Dejen (or Dashen), with a summit at 4533m (14,872ft) elevation.

Kilimanjaro, Tanzania
Mount Kilimanjaro is not only Africa's highest mountain, but with a summit elevation of 5895m (19,341ft) above sea level it is also the world's highest single freestanding mountain. The mountain is actually a dormant volcano with three specific volcanic cones, two of which are extinct but one, Kibo, with the potential for distant future eruptions.

ABOVE:

Tents on Kilimanjaro, Tanzania
At the height of a cruising
aircraft, tents cluster on the
elevated slopes of Kilimanjaro.
Typically, more than 50,000
people attempt to ascend
Kilimanjaro every year.

RIGHT:

Kilimanjaro, Tanzania
Kilimanjaro has multiple routes
to the summit, many of them
open to trekkers rather than
climbers. The mountain's high
altitude, abrasive weather and
challenging slopes, however,
mean that about 40 per cent of
trekkers fail to make the summit.

OPPOSITE:

Dendrosenecio kilimanjari,
Kilimanjaro, Tanzania
Dendrosenecio kilimanjari, a type
of groundsel plant, crowd the
middle elevations of Kilimanjaro,
some growing up to 6m (20ft)
in height. The mountain has five
ecosystems from base to summit,
thus produces a spectacular
range of flora.

ALL PHOTOGRAPHS:

Northern Ice Field, Kilimanjaro, Tanzania
Kilimanjaro's snowy cap, known as the Northern Ice Field, contributes towards its distinctive appearance. Temperatures there can drop as low as -27°C (-17°F).

OVERLEAF:

Kibo Crater, Kilimanjaro, Tanzania
A slightly menacing close-up of the Kibo crater on Kilimanjaro. At its widest point it is 2.4km (1.5 miles) across. The other two craters on the mountain are Mawensi to the east and Shira to the west.

Mount Mawenzi, Kilimanjaro, Tanzania
The third-highest peak in Africa, Mount Mawenzi is the second-highest peak on Kilimanjaro, after the Kibo peak, although at 5149m (16,893ft) the mountain is scarcely in Kibo's shadow. Furthermore, Mawenzi is more difficult and dangerous to climb than Kibo, as its slopes are precipitous and prone to crumbling and rockfalls.

Mount Kenya, Kenya
Like Kilimanjaro, Mount Kenya
is a volcano in origin, although
now it is entirely extinct. It
summits at 5199m (17,056ft)
elevation, making it Africa's
second-highest mountain. It
dominates the surrounding
Mount Kenya National Park
and Reserve, a site of spectacular
ecological diversity and beauty.

OPPOSITE:
Plant Life, Mount Kenya, Kenya
Although Mount Kenya's
upper slopes are mostly barren,
the lower slopes have much
biodiversity. Plant life is watered
by rain and also by the meltwater
from the remnants of 12 glaciers
on the mountain.

ABOVE:
**Sunrise over Mount Kenya,
Kenya**
Sunrise begins to stir over the
summit of Mount Kenya. Visible
here are the top rungs of a
climbing ladder that has been
bolted into the rock's surface to
help trekkers make the summit
without climbing skills.

Mount Karisimbi, Virunga Mountains, Rwanda
Mount Karisimbi is the highest of the Virunga Mountains in east-central Africa, its summit at 4507m (14,787ft). The mountain sits on the border of Congo (Kinshasa) and Rwanda.

Karisimbi Gorilla Family, Mount Karisimbi, Virunga Mountains, Rwanda
The Karisimbi Gorilla Family are a group of about 19 imperilled gorillas that live on the forested slopes of Mount Karisimbi. They are one of several groups that inhabit the Volcanoes National Park in Rwanda.

Mount Karisimbi, Virunga Mountains, Rwanda
The Virunga Mountains are a volcanic range extending approximately 80km (50 miles). There are eight major peaks (Karisimbi is the highest), six of them extinct but two still active.

Mount Stanley, Ruwenzori Range, DRC / Uganda
Mount Stanley is a grand massif straddling the border of the Democratic Republic of Congo (DRC) and Uganda. Those ascending the mountain pass through verdant jungles of primordial beauty.

Margherita Peak, Mount Stanley, Ruwenzori Range, DRC / Uganda
Just visible through the clouds, Mount Stanley's Margherita Peak rises to an elevation of 5119m (16,795ft). As well as being the highest mountain in the DRC and Uganda, Stanley is the third-highest mountain in Africa.

LEFT:
Climbers on Mount Stanley, Ruwenzori Range, DRC / Uganda
Climbers on Mount Stanley stand in its deep snows. Poor visibility can descend literally in minutes at the higher reaches.

OPPOSITE:
Mount Stanley, Ruwenzori Range, DRC / Uganda
Mount Stanley is saturated with rain, snow, sleet, fog and high humidity. However, its atmospherics produce exceptional plant fertility.

Bujuku Valley viewed from Mount Stanley, Ruwenzori Range, DRC / Uganda
A breathtaking view down the Bujuku Valley from the summit of Mount Stanley. Attempting to capture their barren beauty, the Roman mathematician and geographer Ptolemy dubbed the Ruwenzori Mountains the 'Mountains of the Moon'.

Mount Speke, Ruwenzori Range, Uganda
Mount Speke is the second-highest mountain in the Ruwenzori range. It was named after the 19th-century English explorer John Hanning Speke, who spent much time in Africa but never actually climbed the eponymous mountain.

ABOVE:

Mount Speke, Ruwenzori Range, Uganda

Together Mount Speke, Mount Baker and Mount Stanley form a triangle enclosing the Bujuku Valley, a place rich in wildlife and tropical flora. The valley was carved out in prehistory by glaciation; the Ruwenzori Range still features glaciers, albeit of diminishing extent.

RIGHT:

Rockpool, Mount Speke, Ruwenzori Range, Uganda

A rockpool reflects the timeless landscape of Mount Speke. The mountain has four peaks, the highest of which is Vittorio Emanuele at 4890m (16,040ft). The peak was named in 1906 by the mountaineering Duke of Abruzzi after the Italian king Vittorio Emanuele III.

ABOVE:

Drakensberg Mountains, South Africa

The Drakensberg Mountains are a sun-drenched range that runs across southern Africa for a distance of approximately 1126km (700 miles). They are part of the 'Great Escarpment', a long, rocky ridge demarcating Africa's southern coastal strip from its interior plateau.

RIGHT:

Sunrise over Drakensberg Mountains, South Africa

The sun rises over the scenic beauty of Drakensberg. The Khahlamba-Drakensberg Park is designated a UNESCO World Heritage site.

OPPOSITE BOTTOM:

Drakensberg Mountains, South Africa

The highest point in the Drakensberg, and in South Africa, is Mount Thabana Ntlenyana, which reaches 3482m (11,424ft) elevation.

North America

Continental North America is geologically dominated by three major mountain ranges. In the east of the continent, running roughly parallel to the Atlantic coast from eastern Canada to the US state of Alabama, are the Appalachian Mountains. Although the Appalachians are relatively low-lying compared to more soaring ranges (the highest peak in the range is Mount Mitchell at 2037m/6684ft), their temperate forest biome hosts some of North America's richest displays of flora and fauna. The Rocky Mountains in the west, by contrast, includes some of the planet's mightiest snow-capped peaks. The Rockies form the continental divide of the United States (i.e. they determine whether rivers run to the Pacific or the Atlantic) and are the second-longest mountain chain in the world, crossing 4800km (3000 miles) of territory from British Columbia to New Mexico. The highest point in the Rockies is Mount Elbert, at 4401m (14,440ft) elevation. To the west of the Rockies are the Sierra Nevada Mountains, far shorter in overall distance at 640km (400 miles), but abundant in scale and beauty, and including the highest mountain in the lower 48 states (Mount Whitney). Around these three chains run and intersect numerous smaller ranges, making North America an endless bounty for climbers and hikers.

OPPOSITE:
Mount Logan, St Elias Mountains, Yukon, Canada
With a main peak reaching 5959m (19,551ft) in elevation, Mount Logan is the highest peak in Canada and the second-highest peak in North America.

Mount Logan, St Elias Mountains, Yukon, Canada
Mount Logan is a vast massif with 13 major peaks, 11 of them at more than 5000m (16,400ft) elevation. The mountain's higher slopes are wreathed in deep snow, even in the summer months, hence the mountain attracts many 'ski climbers' – those who ascend on foot, but descend at considerable speed and risk on skis.

Mount Logan, St Elias Mountains, Yukon, Canada
This long shot of Mount Logan gives an airy sense of the massif's scale and beauty. The ridge crest of the mountain alone stretches some 16km (10 miles), with the entire mountain more than 32km (20 miles) long. The mountain is the centrepiece of the St Elias Mountains, a major Pacific coast range along the border of Canada and Alaska.

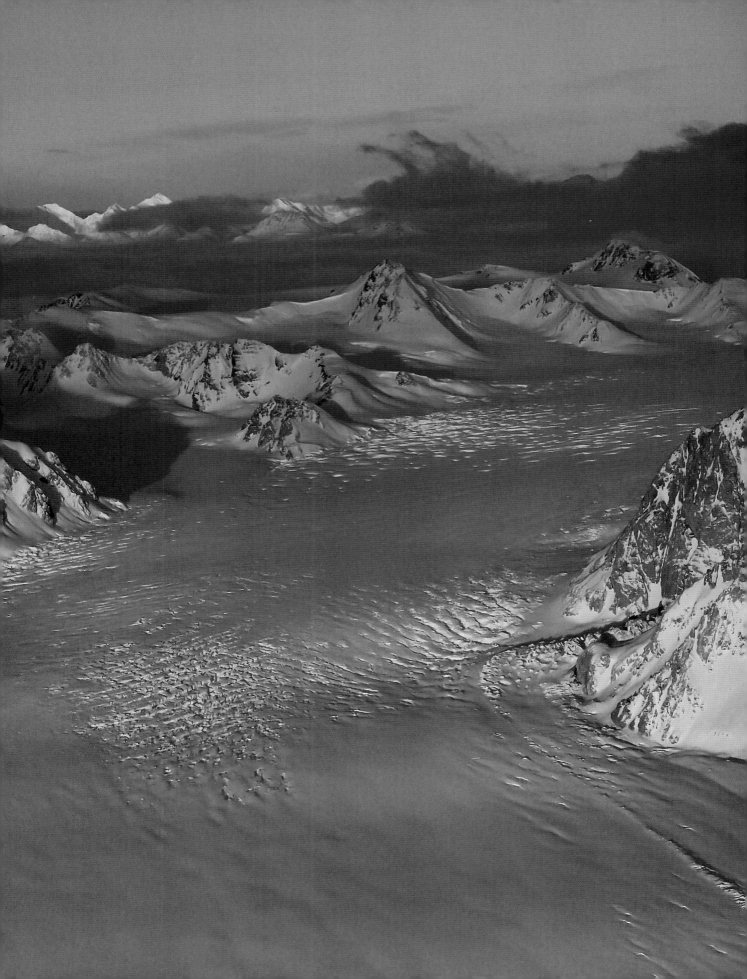

Kaskawulsh Glacier, Kluane National Park, Yukon, Canada
Swirling elegantly through the St Elias Mountains, the Kaskawulsh Glacier is a breathtaking geological feature, approximately 78km (48 miles) long and covering an area of 39,000 sq km (15,000 sq miles). At its broadest point it is 6.4km (4 miles) wide.

Mount Lucania, St Elias Mountains, Yukon, Canada
Another Canadian monster, Mount Lucania is Canada's third-highest mountain, rising to an elevation of 5240m (17,190ft). The St Elias mountains to which it belongs are the second-highest coastal mountain range in the world, after the Andes.

ABOVE:

Mount Lucania, St Elias Mountains, Yukon, Canada
Mount Lucania was given its title in 1897 by the Duke of Abruzzo, who named it after the RMS *Lucania*, the passenger ship on which he sailed from London to New York on his way to a mountaineering expedition on the nearby Mount Saint Elias.

RIGHT:

St Elias Mountains, Kluane National Park, Yukon, Canada
The tracks of a native grizzly bear mark a sandy valley in the Kluane National Park. This unforgiving but beautiful landscape in south-western Yukon features glaciers, forests, lakes and rivers framed by the St Elias Mountains.

TOP:
Air Taxi over St Elias Mountains, Kluane National Park, Yukon, Canada
For those wanting to experience the full beauty of the St Elias Mountains without the legwork, air taxis provide the most convenient means of crossing the peaks and crests.

BOTTOM:
St Elias Mountains, Kluane National Park, Yukon, Canada
Visible from the highway running around nearby Kluane Lake, the St Elias Mountains form a majestic backdrop in the Canadian landscape.

Mount Vancouver, St Elias Mountains, Canada / USA
Nestling on the Canadian-Alaskan border, Mount Vancouver is a three-summit mountain, with its highest northern summit at 4812m (15,787ft) elevation.

Mount Denali, Alaska Range, Alaska, USA
Mount Denali is North America's loftiest peak, with a summit
elevation of 6190m (20,320ft) above sea level. It was formerly known
as Mount McKinley, but following a prolonged naming dispute it was
returned to its original indigenous/Alaskan name of Denali in 2015.

Mount Foraker, Alaska Range, Alaska, USA
Named after Joseph B. Foraker, a 19th-century US senator, Mount Foraker is the third-highest peak in the United States, at 5304m (17,400ft) elevation. Native people refer to the mountain as *Sultana*, regarding it as the 'wife' of Mount Denali.

Mount Saint Elias, St Elias Mountains, Canada / USA
Mount Saint Elias (known in Tinglit as *Yas'éit'aa Shaa* or 'Mountain behind Icy Bay') is the second-highest mountain in both Canada and the United States. Sitting on the Yukon-Alaska border, it has a summit elevation of 5489m (18,008ft). While there are many higher mountains in the world, Saint Elias is regarded as one of the most challenging climbs on the planet, with no straightforward routes to the summit and often lethal weather conditions. There have been scarcely 50 ascents since the first one in 1897.

ABOVE:
Icy Bay, Mount Saint Elias, St Elias Mountains, Canada / USA
Mount Saint Elias seen from across the waters of Icy Bay, which measures more than 48km (30 miles) across. A landslide in the bay in 2015 caused a localized megatsunami that reached a height of 193m (633ft) as it ran up the shore of the bay's Taan Fiord.

RIGHT:
Mount Rainier, Cascade Range, Washington State, USA
Despite its apparent stillness in this photograph, Mount Rainier is an active and dangerous volcano, located about 95km (59 miles) south-southeast of Seattle. The mountain has three named summits, the highest of these being the Columbia Crest at 4392m (14,411ft) elevation.

LEFT:

Mount Rainier, Cascade Range, Washington State, USA
The summer months bring a colourful explosion of life to the lower slopes and valleys of Mount Rainier. The mountain features 26 major glaciers, and summer meltwater irrigates the luxurious subalpine wild flower meadows below.

ABOVE TOP AND BOTTOM:

Deer and Marmot, Mount Rainier, Cascade Range, Washington State, USA
Mount Rainier watches over a plethora of fauna, including a young spotted deer (bottom) and a hoary marmot (top). The mountain's forest, subalpine and alpine zones host more than 65 species of mammal and 182 species of bird.

**Climbers on Mount Rainier,
Cascade Range, Washington
State, USA**
Climbers strain against the slopes
of Mount Rainier as the sunrise
breaks the horizon behind them.
The mountain is a popular North
American climbing destination
with more than 10,000 climbers
attempting to reach the summit
every year.

ALL PHOTOGRAPHS:

El Capitan, Yosemite National Park, California, USA
An astonishing granite block towering above the Yosemite National Park, El Capitan has an elevation above sea level of 2308m (7573ft) from the valley floor. However, it is most famous for its 1100m (3608ft) vertical wall, one of the climbing world's greatest challenges.

El Capitan, Yosemite National Park, California, USA
Early morning sun lights the face of El Capitan. The 'Nose' route of the mountain was first ascended in 1958, but the mountain became particularly famous when, on 3 June 2017, Alex Honnold audaciously completed the first free solo climb (i.e. without the aid of ropes or harnesses).

Half Dome, Sierra Nevada Range, Yosemite National Park, California, USA
Appearing as if split in half by a god-like power, the Half Dome is a granite rock formation in the Yosemite National Park. Geologically, Half Dome is regarded as an *arête*, a narrow blade of rock that forms a ridge between two valleys.

LEFT AND BELOW:
Northwest Face, Half Dome, Sierra Nevada Range, Yosemite National Park, California, USA
An ascent up Half Dome's vertical north-west face is only viable for experienced and professional climbers

OPPOSITE:
Ascent up Half Dome, Sierra Nevada Range, Yosemite National Park, California, USA
Despite its impregnable appearance, Half Dome can be hiked, mainly via the Cable Route around the side of the mountain, named after the double steel cables anchored to the rock that provide grip for the climbers over the final 120m (400ft) to the summit. At peak periods during the summer months, as many as a thousand people a day make this ascent.

Mount Whitney, Sierra Nevada Mountains, California, USA
Tracing the eastern side of California for more than 400km (250 miles), the Sierra Nevada Mountains offer one of the most magnificent landscapes in the United States. Mount Whitney is the range's highest peak at 4418m (14,494ft) above sea level.

ABOVE:
Lone Pine Peak, Sierra Nevada Mountains, California, USA
Lone Pine Peak resides in the southern portion of the Sierra Nevada range. It is an imposing, 3947m (12,949ft) mountain, striking enough to be featured as the default desktop image for Apple's macOS Sierra computer operating system.

RIGHT:
Sierra Nevada Mountains, California, USA
The Sierra Nevada Mountains have a milder, more temperate climate than many other mountain ranges in the United States. This helps to produce the wonderfully inviting landscapes that attract explorers, tourists and settlers alike.

**Twin Lakes, Mount Elbert,
Rocky Mountains, Colorado,
USA**
A panoramic summer-time
view from Twin Lakes across to
Mount Elbert. With an elevation
of 4401m (14,400ft), Mount
Elbert is the highest point in the
Rockies. Despite the elevation, it
can be hiked by anyone with
a good level of fitness.

Mount Mitchell, Black Mountains, North Carolina, USA
With bucolic views over the Black Mountains, Mount Mitchell is the highest peak in North Carolina at 2037m (6684ft). The Black Mountains are in turn part of the iconic Appalachian range, home to some of the greatest forested areas in the United States.

Grand Teton, Teton Range, Wyoming, USA
Located in the Grand Teton National Park, Grand Teton is part of the Teton mountains, a sub-range of the Rocky Mountains. The mountain is a popular climbing destination, offering three main routes to the summit of varying technical difficulty. Some intrepid souls even ski down the mountain during the winter months.

ABOVE:

Teton Range, Wyoming, USA
The Teton Range extends for approximately 64km (40 miles) through the state of Wyoming. The Grand Teton National Park that surrounds the mountains covers an expanse of 1300 sq km (501 sq miles), and is known for being one of the truly untouched wildernesses in the United States.

RIGHT:

Grizzly Bears, Teton Range, Wyoming, USA
A family of grizzly bears wanders through the snow in Grand Teton National Park. Grizzly bears are frequently found in forested valleys and lowland regions around mountains. They prefer riparian habitats (i.e. those around the banks of rivers), where they can fish and hunt.

Teton Range, Wyoming, USA
The mountains visible here are part of what is known as the 'Cathedral Group', which include all the highest peaks of the range, with Grand Teton standing prominently in the centre. To the left of Grand Teton are (from left to right) South Teton, Nez Perce Peak and Middle Teton while to the right are Mount Owen and Teewinot Mountain.

LEFT:

Popocatépetl, Mexico
Just 70km (43 miles) south-east
of Mexico City, Popocatépetl
is an active and threatening
volcano, with eruptions or
emissions on a daily basis over
extended periods. Fittingly, the
name Popocatépetl translates as
'Smoking Mountain'. At 5426m
(17,802ft), it is the second-
highest peak in Mexico.

ABOVE:

Summit of Popocatépetl, Mexico
This image of Popocatépetl taken
from the International Space
Station (ISS) shows the snow on
the summit clearly framing the
volcano's crater, which measures
400 × 600m (1312 × 1968ft).
In recent years, the volcano
has been making an average of
54 gas and ash emissions daily,
alongside frequent tremours.

Pico de Orizaba / Citlaltépetl, Mexico

Dormant since 1687, the soaring volcano of Pico de Orizaba – also known as Citlaltépetl – is the third-highest peak in North America at an elevation of 5610m (18,406ft). The mountain is a popular destination for climbers, who typically make the ascent during the better weather between October and March.

South America

We cannot separate South America from its greatest geological feature: the Andes Mountains. The Andes are the backbone of South America, stretching an unbroken 8900km (5500 miles) from the Caribbean Sea at coastal Venezuela to the southern tip of the continent in southern Chile and Argentina. Across that distance, the Andes form a staggering natural vista of dizzying peaks, sweeping valleys, high-altitude plateaus and sky-ripping ridgelines. The densest concentration of the highest peaks is found in the northern half of the Andes just to the east of the Atacama Desert, where the average terrain elevation above sea level is more than 3000m (9842ft), but with numerous peaks above the 5000m (16,404ft) and 6000m (19,684ft) marks. The highest of the Andes, however, nestle further south along the border between Argentina and Chile, the greatest of them being Mount Aconcagua, the highest point in the Western hemisphere. Yet, the Andes are far from the only South American range. Others include the Sierra Nevada de Santa Marta in northern Colombia, the Serra do Mar and Mantiqueira Mountains in Brazil and the Wilhelminagebergte in central Suriname. Collectively, South America's mountains frame the mighty Amazon basin, together forming a continent of unparalleled beauty.

OPPOSITE:
Mount Fitz Roy, South Patagonic Andes, Patagonia
Mount Fitz Roy is one of the world's most challenging climbs. It is named after Robert Fitz Roy, the captain of HMS *Beagle*, the vessel that famously transported Charles Darwin on his round-the-world survey voyage in 1831–36.

Mount Fitz Roy, South Patagonic Andes, Patagonia
Mount Fitz Roy is known by several other names, including Cerro Fitzroy, Cerro Chaltel and Chaltén. It stands in the Los Glaciares National Park and straddles the border between Argentina and Chile. At 3375m (11,073ft) elevation it is the highest in a range of granite peaks.

Pico Cristóbal Colón, Colombia
The highest of Colombia's peaks at 5730m (18,800ft), Pico Cristóbal Colón sits in the far north of the country, the most elevated point for nearly 1300km (807 miles). The mountain is named after the famous Italian explorer of the Renaissance, Christopher Columbus.

ABOVE TOP:
Summits of Aconcagua,
Principal Cordillera,
Andes, Argentina
Aconcagua stakes its claim in
global geology to being the
highest point in the Western
hemisphere, at 6959m (22,831ft).
It has north and south summits,
the two peaks connected by the
Cresta del Guanaco, a 1-km
(0.6-mile) ridge.

ABOVE BOTTOM:
Aconcagua,
Principal Cordillera,
Andes, Argentina
To indigenous people, Aconcagua
has long been regarded as a
sacred place. An expedition
in 1985 found the mummified
remains of a seven-year-old
boy who had been sacrificed as
part of an Inca ritual, 5300m
(17,388ft) above sea level

RIGHT:
Trekkers on Aconcagua,
Principal Cordillera,
Andes, Argentina
Aconcagua is one of the world's
'Seven Summits', but it is also a
mountain that can be ascended,
at least via its northern route,
without the need for equipment
such as ropes and pins. Altitude
sickness, however, can be an
obstacle for many trekkers.

Pico Paraná, Serra do Mar Range, Brazil
Located in Paraná State, Campina Grande do Sul County, Pico Paraná is Brazil's highest mountain. It is known as a peak of astonishing natural beauty, its rocky summit giving way to lush tropical slopes and valleys below.

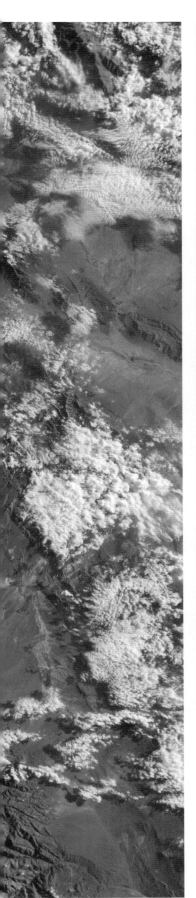

LEFT:

Andes, South America
The Andes Mountains – here
photographed from the orbiting
International Space Station (ISS)
– are one of the planet's boldest
geological features. Although
the Andes can be regarded as
a single massive range, they
are rationalized into a series of
separate ranges, or cordilleras,
at various points along their
length.

ABOVE:

**Cordillera Oriental,
Andes, South America**
One of the major divisions
of the Andes is between the
eastern and western ranges,
known respectively as the
Cordillera Oriental and the
Cordillera Occidental. On a
north–south axis, the mountains
are also divided into Northern,
Central and Southern (or
Patagonian) Andes.

Mount Huascarán, Andes, Peru
With its summit at 6768m
(22,205ft), Mount Huascarán is
Peru's highest mountain. Despite
its popularity with climbers, it
has a dark history. An avalanche
in 1962 killed 3500 people in the
valley below, but an earthquake
on 31 May 1970 caused a large
portion of the northern side of
the mountain to collapse, the
resulting landslides burying
several major urban zones and
killing as many as 25,000 people.

Huascarán National Park, Cordillera Blanca, Peru
The Huascarán National Park covers an area of 3400 sq km (1312 sq miles) in the Central Andes. As well Mount Huascarán, which lends the park its name, the park has multiple high-altitude peaks, including several reaching above 6000m (19,684ft), such as Mount Copa and Mount Huantsán.

LEFT:

**Licancabur,
Andean Volcanic Belt, Andes,
Bolivia / Chile**
A prominent volcanic cone
on the border of Chile and
Bolivia, Licancabur reaches an
elevation of 5916m (19,409ft).
At its summit is a lake measuring
roughly 90 × 70m (295 × 230ft).
One of the world's highest lakes,
it is rich in rare planktonic fauna.

ABOVE:

**Summit of Licancabur, Andean
Volcanic Belt, Andes,
Bolivia / Chile**
Snows can cover the slopes of
Licancabur, where temperatures
at the summit swing between
5 to -40°C (41 to -40°F). The
mountain is typically very sunny
and dry, so snows can disappear
quickly apart from at the very
summit or in sheltered areas.

Mount Mercedario, Cordillera de la Ramada, Andes, Argentina
With a summit at 6710m (22,014ft), Mount Mercedario is the eighth-highest mountain in South America, and stands just 100km (62 miles) north of Aconcagua. It is known for being a pristine wilderness, with only small numbers of climbers and trekkers tackling it each year.

LEFT:

Alpacas, Andes
Even at extremes of temperature and altitude, nature always finds a way in the Andes. Hardy alpacas are farmed for their fleece and meat. These resilient creatures can thrive at Andean altitudes of 3500 to 5000m (11,000 to 16,000ft) above sea level.

ABOVE TOP:

Andean Condor, Andes
Weighing up to 15kg (33lb) and with a wingspan of 3.2m (10ft 6in), the Andean Condor is a masterpiece of evolution. It can glide for hours without flapping its wings and at altitudes of 4572m (15,000ft), while being able to spot an animal carcass miles below.

ABOVE BOTTOM:

Ojos del Salado, Andes, Argentina / Chile
A dormant complex volcano rather than a single mountain, Ojos del Salado has a highest peak reaching 6893m (22,615ft) in elevation. This photograph captures the mountain's aridity, with very little precipitation over the course of each year.

Picture Credits